SURFBOARDS

From Start to Finish

Ryan A. Smith

Photographs by Devon Howard

BLACKBIRCH PRESS

An imprint of Thomson Gale, a part of The Thomson Corporation

THOMSON

GALE™

WITHDRAWN

Det...   London • Munich

Dedication: To Mother Nature and all the waves crashing on Earth.

© 2006 Thomson Gale, a part of The Thomson Corporation.
Thomson and Star Logo are trademarks and Gale and Blackbirch Press are registered trademarks used herein under license.

For more information, contact
Blackbirch Press
27500 Drake Rd.
Farmington Hills, MI 48331-3535
Or you can visit our Internet site at www.gale.com

Photo Credits: Cover, all photos © Devon Howard, except page 3 © Divine/A-Frame; pages 4 (inset), 31 (main) © Ryan A. Smith; page 11 © Marisa Breyer; page 31 (inset) Courtesy of The Greenroom

Special Thanks: Special thanks to Blackbirch Press editor Marla Felkins Ryan; Rich Pavel; Peter, Jean-Paul, and Sally St. Pierre; Devon Howard; Gary Stuber; Mark Donnellan; Marlon Bacon; Josh Englund; the Whitehead brothers; the Copeman brothers; and Kenny Mann for making this book possible.

LIBRARY OF CONGRESS CATALOGING-IN-PUBLICATION DATA

Smith, Ryan A., 1974–
   Surfboards / by Ryan A. Smith.
      p. cm. — (Made in the USA)
   Includes bibliographical references and index.
   ISBN 1-4103-0728-X (hard cover : alk. paper) 1. Surfboards—Juvenile literature. I. Title. II. Series: Made in the U.S.A.
GV840.S8S65 2006
797.3'2—dc22
                                              2005028762

Contents

Surfboards

Surfing was invented by the ancient Polynesians more than 1,000 years ago. Respected craftsmen in South Pacific island chains including Hawaii, Tahiti, and the Marquesas hand carved heavy surfboards out of native woods like koa and wiliwili. Originally, surf-boards were made only for members of the Polynesian royalty. Kings, queens, princes, and princesses were the first to ride them great distances along the beautiful waves of the tropical region.

Modern surfboards are made by teams of skilled men and women using space-age materials.

Today surfboards are available to everyone at stores around the world. Teams of skilled men and women build surfboards using a combination of lightweight, space-age materials. Some large factories can construct hundreds of surfboards every month.

But how exactly are surfboards made?

Greenroom Surfboards

Greenroom Surfboards is a popular surfboard company based in San Diego, California. Its owner, Rich Pavel, has been shaping, or carving, surfboards out of wood and foam for more than 30 years. Pavel is also the main surfboard designer for Greenroom Surfboards. He makes hundreds of surfboards every year.

Since 1970 Rich Pavel has shaped thousands of boards for the Greenroom Surfboards label.

Foam Blanks

Most surfboards begin as large blocks of ridged polyurethane foam called blanks. Blanks are formed inside large molds with a combination of heat, pressure, and chemical reactions. Strips of wood, called stringers, run lengthwise down the centers of the blanks.

Most surfboards begin as bulky, polyurethane foam surfboard blanks.

Skinning the Blank

Once the blank is delivered, the shaper lays it onto a set of floor racks to make sure it is perfectly level. The shaper also makes sure that the blank is the desired length, width, and outline for the chosen surfboard design.

A shaper uses a power planer (inset) to skin the layer of crust from the foam blank.

To begin shaping, the shaper must remove the thin outermost layer of the blank, called the crust. The crust is rougher than the soft, white foam inside the blank. Carefully walking back and forth along both sides of the entire length of the blank, the shaper uses a handheld machine called a power planer to shave off, or skin, a thin layer of crust.

The power planer is a woodworking tool that has small spinning blades that accurately cut sections from the foam and stringer wood. The shaper first skins the top of the blank, called the deck, and then turns it over and skins the bottom. After the blank is completely skinned, the shaper continues to shave it to attain the desired thickness.

The shaper removes the blank's crust in order to work with the soft foam found inside.

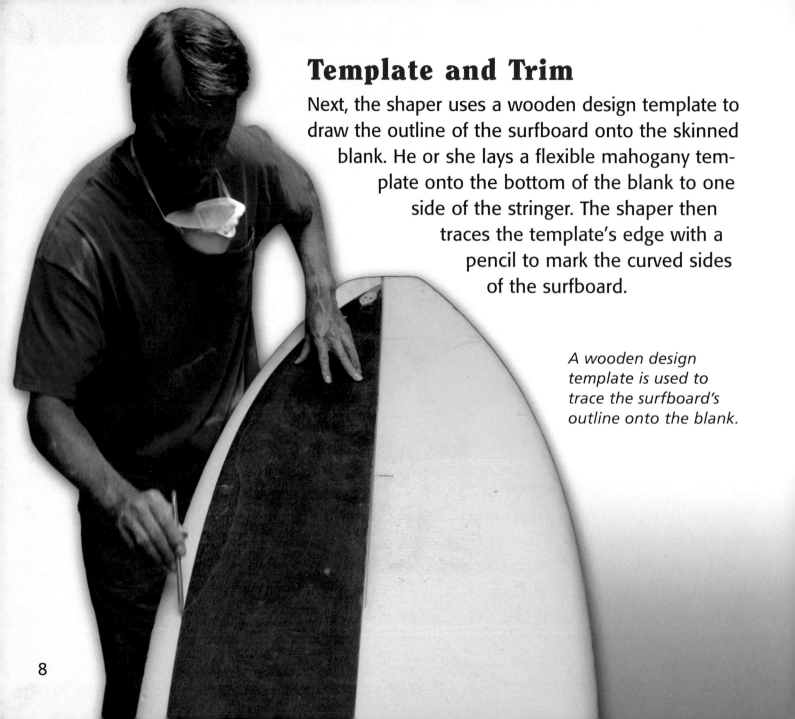

Template and Trim

Next, the shaper uses a wooden design template to draw the outline of the surfboard onto the skinned blank. He or she lays a flexible mahogany template onto the bottom of the blank to one side of the stringer. The shaper then traces the template's edge with a pencil to mark the curved sides of the surfboard.

A wooden design template is used to trace the surfboard's outline onto the blank.

He or she turns over the template, placing it on the opposite side of the stringer, and traces again in the same way. This creates a perfectly symmetrical outline of the surfboard on the blank. With the pencil outline as a guide, the shaper uses a handsaw to trim excess foam from the sides.

The shaper cuts the excess foam from the sides of the blank with a handsaw.

There are an estimated 2 million surfers riding waves worldwide.

Foiling the Foam

The blank is still bulky at this stage. Now the shaper uses the power planer to scoop curve into the bottom of the blank. This process is called foiling the blank.

Curve is added from the front, or nose, down the blank and through the tail end. This curve is called rocker. The rocker helps make the surfboard more maneuverable.

Curve, or rocker, is scooped into the bottom of the blank with a power planer.

Modern Surfboard Designs

Pavel produces a wide variety of board designs for Greenroom Surfboards. Each type of surfboard performs differently. Some are made for specific sizes or types of waves, as well as for riders with different skill levels. For instance, a long and wide surfboard is best suited for slow, small waves and begin-ning surfers. A thin and short surfboard is made for

fast, challenging waves and amateur or professional surfers. Some surfboards are built specifically to handle breathtaking speeds while riding giant 50-foot (15m) waves while other boards might be designed to turn smoother on small waves or to paddle easier.

The Rails

Properly shaping the two sides of the blank, called the rails, is one of the most important steps in surfboard building. A surfboard's rails help it to ride smoothly and also help the board gain momentum from the power of a wave.

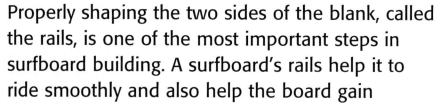

The shaper moves the power planer back and forth along the rails shaving long, thick layers of foam from it. The two rails must be made as equal in curve and thickness as possible. This makes the deck slightly dome shaped at the rails. The domed effect helps reduce drag.

The blank's two rails must be made as equal in curve and thickness as possible.

To refine the rails, the shaper uses a series of sanding techniques. A very abrasive sanding block is first wiped across the rails and deck to make minor adjustments to the blank. Then the shaper uses a second, smaller block to remove the ridges left by the power planer. Finally, he or she pulls a sheet of coarse sandpaper up and down both rails several times to make them smooth and equal.

From top to bottom: A power planer creates the dome-shaped effect along both rails. A series of abrasive sanding blocks removes the tiny ridges left by the planer. The finished curve of the rails will allow the surfboard to ride smoothly.

Sanding into Shape

After the blank has been shaped roughly into the desired design and dimensions, the shaper uses finer sandpaper and sanding screens to carefully shape it further. The sandpaper and screens are used one at a time to remove any slight bumps on the rails, nose, or deck of the blank. Progressively finer grades of sandpaper are used until the blank is ready to finish.

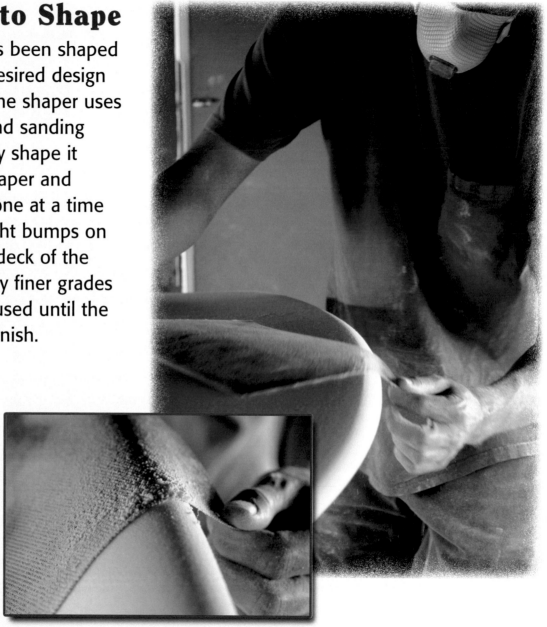

Sanding screens (main and inset) remove any slight bumps from the blank's rails.

14

Thinning the Stringer

Because the sanding process wears down the blank's foam, the wooden stringer in the center now rises above the surface. To fix this, the shaper pushes and pulls small woodworking planers along the center, shaving the wood down until the entire stringer is level with the surrounding foam.

A small woodworking planer shaves thin layers from the wooden stringer.

Finishing Touches

The shaper makes a few finishing touches to the blank before moving it to the next phase of surfboard building. The bottom edge and deck curve of the tail are refined at this stage using a delicate finishing sandpaper and screen. Shaping the tail properly helps the board perform consistently. Now the blank is smooth and refined.

Once the blank is finished, the shaper calculates where the fins will work best for the surfboard design and draws pencil lines to mark the areas. Lastly, as a mark of authenticity, the shaper signs the blank near the stringer with a pencil. The blank is then carefully wrapped in a long plastic bag and delivered to the glassing factory.

Opposite (From top to bottom): *The tail design of the surfboard blank is refined by hand. Pencil lines marking the correct fin placement are added to the bottom of the blank. Finally, the shaper signs the blank along the stringer.*

On this page: *Shaped foam surfboard blanks are shipped to a glassing factory once they are completed.*

The Glassing Factory

The Moonlight Glassing Company in San Diego glasses many of Pavel's Greenroom Surfboards. At the glassing factory, a foam blank is given a hard, protective shell. This shell keeps water from soaking in and weakening the foam. Glassing also enables the surfboard to glide on the water's surface.

Foam surfboard blanks are given hard, protective shells at factories like Moonlight Glassing Company.

Custom Airbrush

Often the glassing process begins in the airbrush room. Here, artists paint custom color schemes or artwork directly onto some blanks. Anything from a solid color or stripes to a cartoon illustration—or even a surfer's portrait—can be painted onto the blank.

Water-based paints are combined to achieve the correct color and a thin consistency. An artist lightly sprays steady streams of paint onto the blank with a handheld airbrush machine. Once the color work is finished, the painted blank is carefully placed onto a set of horizontal racks to dry. Airbrushing complicated artwork onto a blank can take several hours.

An artist applies steady streams of water-based paint to the bottom of a blank.

Laminating the Blank

Sealing the shaped blank begins in the laminating room. The laminator prepares a precise mixture of polyester laminating resin, a chemical catalyst, and sometimes color pigments inside a paper bucket. The laminator must measure the ingredients carefully to make sure the mixture hardens at exactly the perfect time. If too much catalyst is used, the laminating coat will harden too quickly and become brittle. If too little catalyst is used, the glassing will harden too slowly and become gummy.

A laminator uses a squeegee to spread a mixture of resin, catalyst, and blue pigment into the fiberglass cloth.

The laminator cuts long sheets of fiberglass cloth to size, drapes them over the entire blank, and then pours on the laminating resin mixture. The laminator has only a few minutes to apply the resin before it thickens. Using a squeegee, the laminator spreads the mixture evenly across one entire side of the blank to bond the foam, fiberglass, and resin together. He or she is careful to remove air bubbles trapped in the cloth and cover any exposed foam.

The same process is applied to the bottom of the blank, but this time the laminator tucks the edges of the cloth around the rails to the deck. The board is then left to dry.

Sheets of fiberglass cloth help the foam blank bond to the resin mixture, and give the surfboard a lot of its strength.

Hot Coating the Deck

Once the first layer is dry, another layer of resin is applied to the laminated surfboard. The resin used at this stage is hot and, as it dries, becomes much harder than the laminating resin. Another difference between the two resin layers is that no fiberglass cloth or paint is used during hot coating.

The hot coater pours the hot-coat resin onto the deck of the surfboard. Moving very quickly, he or she uses a paintbrush to fill and seal the weave of the fiberglass cloth. The entire deck of the surfboard is covered evenly and smoothly and then allowed to dry.

A room filled with laminated surfboards is set up for hot coats of resin.

Above: Using a paintbrush, the hot coater evenly fills the weave of the fiberglass cloth.

23

Fins

Every modern surfboard built today has fins attached to the bottom side of the tail. Fins are attached after the hot-coat resin on the deck dries. The board is set upside down on racks so the fin pencil markings left by the shaper are visible. These marks show the exact places and angles at which the fins must be attached.

First, thin lines of hot-coat resin and catalyst are brushed over the pencil marks. The fins are erected perfectly into place by hand, directly on top of the resin lines. The resin lightly sticks the fins to the surfboard to keep them standing. Then small pieces of fiberglass rope and cloth are quickly fixed to both sides of the fins with a thick coat of laminating resin. The rope, cloth, and laminating resin strongly bond the fins to the board and make them sturdy. As the mix hardens any excess fiberglass cloth and resin are carefully removed with a razor blade. Finally, the entire bottom of the surfboard is brushed with a layer of hot-coat resin and left to dry.

Top Left: The fins are set into place, directly on top of the pencil marks.

Some surfboards are fitted with an advanced fin system that allows the surfer to install a series of different fins that each changes the board's performance. Fin systems also allow the surfer to completely remove the fins, making the surfboard easier to carry on airplanes.

Above Right: Fiberglass cloth and a resin mixture help bond the fins to the surfboard's tail.

Bottom Left: A razor blade is used to trim excess cloth and resin from the fins as the mixture hardens.

25

Sanding

After the hot coat is thoroughly dry, the surfboard is sanded. Sanding helps refine the glassed surfboard close to the design intended by the shaper. Any tiny ridges and bumps left on the surface from the hot-coat process are also sanded down with coarse sandpaper and a powerful circular sanding machine.

A sanding machine is used to flatten any bumps or flaws on the surface of the surfboard.

The sanding machine spins sandpaper at a speed of 3,000 revolutions per minute (RPMs). The surfboard's deck, bottom, nose, tail, and rails are all machine sanded until the board is symmetrical and any bumps are as smooth as possible. After the machine is used to sand the deck and bottom coats smooth, the rails and fins are sanded by hand.

The delicate edges and angles near the fins and tail must be carefully sanded by hand.

The Gloss Coat

A third and final layer of resin and catalyst, called the gloss coat, is applied to the surfboard to give it a shiny, glossy look. The gloss-coat resin also waterproofs and seals the surfboard.

The gloss-coat mixture is poured first onto the bottom and evenly applied with a paintbrush. Then, once the bottom is dry, the board is turned over and the deck is covered in the same manner. Then the surfboard is left to dry one last time.

Gloss-coat resin is brushed evenly across the deck. The gloss coat waterproofs and seals the surfboard.

Sand and Wet Sand

A surfboard must look good whether someone uses it to ride waves or hangs it on a wall. Surfboard sanders and polishers at Moonlight Glassing take special pride in ensuring that the product of everyone's teamwork leaves the factory in perfect condition.

Another process at the end of the glassing stage makes each board beautiful. First, the sanding machine removes the faint brush marks left on the surface during the gloss coat. A very fine grade of sandpaper makes the surface as flawless as possible while not sanding off too much resin.

Next, the surfboard is wet sanded by hand with water and special sandpaper. This makes the board as smooth as possible. The smoother the board is, the better it will ride a wave.

A surfboard is wet sanded by hand to help make its surface as smooth as possible.

Surfboards are polished with a buffing machine to make them shine.

Polishing

Finally the surfboard is buffed and polished with a high-powered buffing machine. The polisher passes the machine across the entire board, like waxing a car, until every inch of it shines. Perfectly polished surfboards are then packaged safely and ready to be delivered to Pavel's surf shop, The Greenroom.

The Surf Shop

Many of Pavel's new surfboards are sold at The Greenroom surf shop in San Diego. Racks, rows, and rotating stands are filled to the roof with colorful boards of every design and size. Surfers from across the United States, Japan, Europe, and Australia cannot wait to get their Greenroom Surfboards and hit the waves!

Once completely glassed, surfboards of every design, shape, and size are sold to surfers around the world.

The Greenroom
EST. 1970 · Kauai

Glossary

Authenticity Genuineness or realness

Catalyst A substance that causes or speeds up a chemical reaction

Deck The top of a surfboard

Fiberglass A material consisting of fine particles of glass that are woven into a fabric

Laminating Constructing from layers of materials bonded together

Nose The front end, or tip, of a surfboard

Polyurethane A type of foam used in the production of modern surfboards

Rail The side of a surfboard

Resin A transparent, liquid substance that creates the hard, waterproof exterior of a surfboard when mixed with a catalyst

Squeegee A rubber blade used for spreading or wiping liquid material on, across, or off a surface

Symmetrical The same on either side of a center line

Tail The back end of a surfboard

For More Information

Books

Matt Warshaw, *The Encyclopedia of Surfing*. San Diego: Harcourt, 2003.

Doug Werner, *Surfer's Start-Up: A Beginner's Guide to Surfing*. Chula Vista, CA: Tracks Publishing, 1999.

Web Sites

Howabunga (www.signonsandiego.com/uniontrib/20050622/images/quest.pdf). A guide explaining the science of surfing waves.

Legendary Surfers (www.LegendarySurfers.com). A definitive history of surfing, surfboards, surfers, and surf culture.

Index